THE NEW PLANT LIBRARY

FUCHSIAS

THE NEW PLANT LIBRARY

FUCHSIAS

ANDREW MIKOLAJSKI

Consultants: Antony and Norma Wheeler
Photography by Peter Anderson

LORENZ BOOKS

NEW YORK • LONDON • SYDNEY • BATH

This edition published in 1997 by Lorenz Books
27 West 20th Street, New York, New York 10011

LORENZ BOOKS are available for bulk purchase for sales promotion and
for premium use. For details, write or call the manager of special sales:
Lorenz Books, 27 West 20th Street, New York, New York 10011;
(212) 807-6739

Lorenz Books is an imprint of Anness Publishing Limited

ISBN 1 85967 387 2

Publisher: Joanna Lorenz
Senior Editor: Clare Nicholson
Designer: Michael Morey

Printed and bound in Hong Kong

1 3 5 7 9 10 8 6 4 2

Contents

Introduction

*F*rom the elegance of the species to the razzle-dazzle of the showiest modern hybrid, fuchsias are unrivaled as the star performers of summer. In flower from late spring to autumn, and sometimes beyond, they are justifiably popular as some of the most reliable and rewarding of all plants available to modern gardeners. This book aims to open the door on this ever-fascinating genus for those new to the subject and to explain some of the ways in which the plants can be enjoyed. It will also delight the already committed enthusiast with its photographic portraits of some of the most beautiful fuchsias in cultivation.

■ RIGHT
Fuchsias in full bloom provide a wonderful display all summer long.

The history of the fuchsia

At around the beginning of the 18th century, the intrepid French missionary Father Charles Plumier was in Santo Domingo in the West Indies. There, he stumbled on the plant which he later named Fuchsia in honor of the German botanist Leonhard Fuchs (1501–66), who had held the chair of medicine at the University of Tübingen. He can scarcely have realized that he had discovered a plant that would give so much pleasure the world over. However, he created a botanical conundrum that is unresolved to this day.

He published a description of the plant in *Nova Plantarum Americanum Genera* in 1703 under the name *Fuchsia triphylla flore coccinea* (fuchsia with three leaves and red flowers). Modern conventions of nomenclature require that species are defined by two names only, the genus name (in this case *Fuchsia*) and its species epithet, and scholars argue as to whether the plant Father Plumier discovered was either of those known

■ LEFT
A collection of fuchsias that includes a triphylla type with velvety leaves and a golden-leaved hybrid.

■ RIGHT
Hardy species fuchsias trained against pillars: an effective method of display in a mild climate.

today respectively as *F. triphylla,* native to the foothills of Santo Domingo, or the Brazilian *F. coccinea*. Later botanists added to the confusion: Pierre Joseph Redouté made an illustration of a plant grown by the Empress Josephine that he labeled *F. magellanica* (a hardy species that is found in Chile and Argentina) but that looks much more like *F. coccinea.*

Plumier's discovery did not excite much curiosity outside the academic world, and it was not until 1773, when the American William Hogg sent actual specimens of *F. triphylla* to Kew Gardens in Britain, that interest in the genus really began. Additional species were found in Central and South America and also in New Zealand and Tahiti. Most species, however, hail from high on the western slopes of the Andes and grow in cool, damp, densely forested areas where light levels are generally low. Some of these species make good garden plants (though most need greenhouse protection in cold climates), but the majority have specific cultivation requirements that make them attractive to only the dedicated enthusiast. The most significant finds, as far as amateur gardeners are concerned, were *F. magellanica, F. coccinea* and

F. fulgens from Mexico; it is from crosses of these that most of the cultivars we enjoy in gardens today were developed.

It was not until the 1830s, however, when *F. fulgens* was introduced, that breeding fuchsias commercially became a viable proposition, and hybridization began in earnest, mainly in Britain and France. The first large-flowered

hybrids were available by the end of the 1840s, and by the turn of the century the fuchsia had reached its first peak of popularity. Between the two world wars, interest waned in Europe; meanwhile, American breeders took up the gauntlet, and by the 1950s a new wave of hybrids began to make its way across the Atlantic. Since then, the fuchsia has continued to rise in popularity.

Fuchsias as garden plants

Few other plants available today cover themselves in flowers quite so completely, or over quite such a long period, as do fuchsias. Double or single, tubular and elegant or flamboyantly showy, ranging from a blanched, almost white, pastel pink to rich purples, reds and oranges, the flower shapes and colors of the fuchsia of today offer the gardener unlimited possibilities.

Tender fuchsias have become the bedding plant *par excellence*, enjoyed in formal parks and gardens the world over. So vast is the range of tender fuchsias that it is easy to overlook the many hardy types. Often less showy, these can be integrated into mixed borders where, given proper attention, they will give pleasure for many years.

Hardy fuchsias

Hardy fuchsias are shrubby plants that generally survive a winter temperature of 23°F, lower after a long, hot summer. In cool climates, however, they usually behave almost like herbaceous perennials, dying back completely in autumn and producing new growth from the base the following spring.

Hardy fuchsias have various uses in the garden. They integrate well with other plants, and are particularly valued for their late flowering season (usually late summer through to autumn). Some, particularly the species, are useful as specimens in lawns, naturally making elegant mounds with a minimum of pruning. Others may be planted as an informal hedge, though in cool climates these will be deciduous, and cannot be used to make a permanent barrier. There are also many small hardy fuchsias that make their mark in shady rock gardens. Some hardy fuchsias also make good container plants and may be trained as standards.

Tender fuchsias

Tender fuchsias will not survive temperatures below the freezing point and can be used only for permanent outdoor plantings in frost-free climates. In cool climates, therefore, they are used either for summer bedding or for growing in containers or hanging baskets, and are either discarded at the end of the growing season or overwintered under cover. A huge number of cultivars is available.

Bush fuchsias have an upright habit and make good bedding plants. Trailing fuchsias, with long, lax stems, are best in hanging baskets, where the flowers will hang at eye level.

Growing in containers

Many hardy fuchsias, and all tender ones, are suitable for growing in containers. An advantage of growing tender fuchsias in containers in cold climates is that they can be brought into growth under glass in early spring, and will thus flower much earlier than the bedding plants that are available in garden centers around mid-spring (see Buying fuchsias). It is easier to monitor the growth of plants in containers, and many lend themselves to being pruned and trained into shapes that are both attractive in themselves and will

■ BELOW
A collection of showy modern hybrids in a window box.

produce a greater profusion of flowers than plants that are grown in the open border. It is easier than you think to train standards – which can look spectacular when used as "dot" plants – and you can produce a flowering specimen within two years. Bush fuchsias will produce a rounded, lollipop-like head; trailing fuchsias will have a weeping head.

Planting suggestions

Some hardy fuchsias make elegant plants that can stand alone as specimens or be the dominant plant in a mixed border. *F. magellanica* can be grown as a hedge and would be a dazzling backdrop to a late-summer planting of brilliant red cactus dahlias, cannas or *Crocosmia* 'Lucifer.'

It is also useful for coastal gardens as it tolerates exposed sites and high winds. As a specimen in a mixed border, it would add sparks to the blaze of autumn leaf color provided by *Photinia villosa, Cotinus coggygria* or *Parrotia persica* and complement perfectly the shiny red stems of *Euphorbia stricta*. Bronze fennel (*Foeniculum vulgare* 'Purpureum')

■ BELOW
A thickly planted basket for maximum
impact: pastel-hued fuchsias combine with
lobelias, petunias and nemesias.

would look good, too. The cultivar
'Riccartonii' is hardier than the type,
and there is also an attractive but less
vigorous variegated form, *F. m.*
'Variegata' that, with its gray-green
foliage marked with pink and cream,
combines well with late-flowering,
pastel-colored roses.

Other hardy fuchsias include
'Phyllis,' suitable for a hedge in a
sheltered spot, and 'Genii,' with
golden-green foliage that is a
striking feature even before the
flowers emerge. You could team the
latter with shade-loving perennials
such as hostas, perhaps 'Sum and
Substance,' that have similarly colored
leaves. Fill in the gaps in the winter
border with early-flowering bulbs that
will have died down by the time the
fuchsia is due for pruning (see
Pruning a hardy fuchsia). In mild
climates, adventurous gardeners could
try training *F. excorticata* against a
warm wall (see Training a fan). In
frost-free gardens, *F. triphylla,* or any
of its near relatives, makes a splendid
specimen plant.

Bedding fuchsias can be combined
with other bedding plants such as
lobelias, salvias, African marigolds
(*Tagetes*) and *alyssum.* For a subtle,
restful scheme, choose pastel-colored
subjects such as 'Harry Gray' (white

tinged with pink) and combine them
with white lobelias and *alyssum,* or be
more daring and use the stunning
'Thalia' (bright orange-scarlet flowers
and bronze foliage) *en masse* edged
with African marigolds. 'Swingtime,'
treated as a standard, would look
great with its red-and-white flowers
cascading down above a sea of deep
blue lobelias.

In hanging baskets, combine
fuchsias with other trailing plants
such as ivies, begonias or trailing
lobelias, or those that have a
branching habit, such as busy Lizzies

(*Impatiens*). If the basket is in sun for
some of the day, you could also try
the purple-leaved *Tradescantia
pallida,* which is usually grown as a
houseplant. This would be very good
with pink-flowered fuchsias such as
'Jack Shahan' or 'Pink Galore,' or you
could go for a sensational clash by
combining the cherry-red 'Marinka'
with the *Tradescantia* and some
brilliant orange nasturtiums. Another
possibility is the variegated spider
plant (*Chlorophytum comosum*
'Vittatum') which is also usually
grown as a houseplant.

The fuchsia plant

In the wild, fuchsias are mainly evergreen shrubs of varying habit. Some, such as *F. procumbens* from New Zealand, have stems that creep along the ground. Others (e.g. *F. excorticata,* also from New Zealand) eventually make trees over 30 feet in height. A third group, including the Brazilian *F. alpestris* and *F. coccinea,* develops a climbing habit where conditions demand it. A curiosity is the Mexican *F. fulgens,* which has a thick, fleshy, tuberous root like a dahlia. Some species hold their flowers erect; others hang their heads down gracefully. Most species fuchsia flowers are small and dainty, however, and only the hardy *F. magellanica* has become a common garden plant – to such an extent that it is found naturalized throughout South America, eastern Africa, New Zealand and even Ireland. Some fuchsias in the wild produce edible, if unpalatable, fruit.

Modern hybrids mostly carry their leaves in opposite pairs along the stems, but some produce a stem that has its leaves in threes, and it is from these stems that most nurserymen today try and increase their stock – the resulting plants also have leaves in threes, and will be more compact and vigorous than those propagated from two-leaved stems.

Fuchsia flowers vary in their shape and size – ranging from tiny to 3 inches across – but all have certain characteristics in common. Botanically, the flower stalk is known as the pedicel. At the base of the flower is an elongated dome-shaped swelling, the ovary, from which extends a similar section of varying length called the tube. This supports

Stem with leaves in pairs

Stem with leaves in threes

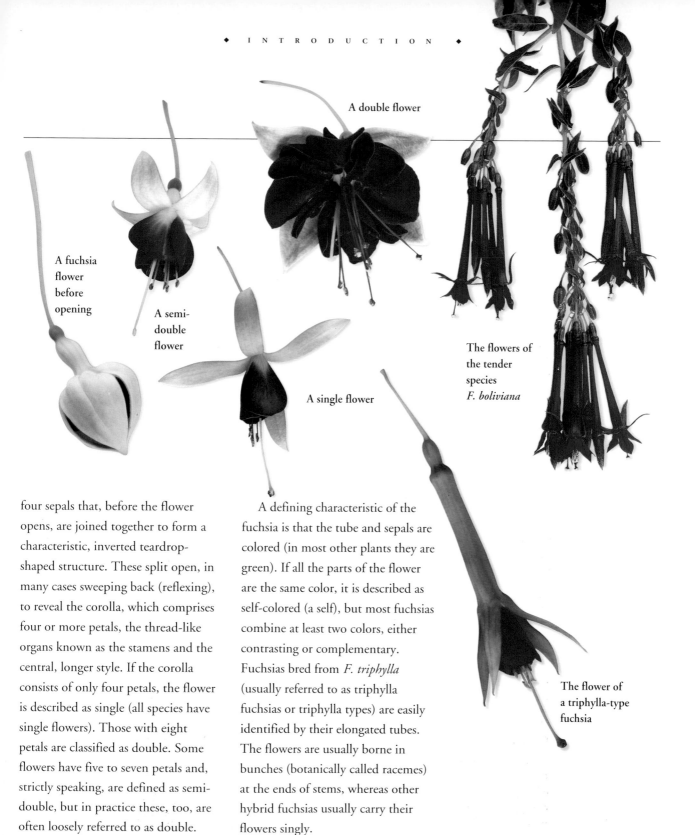

A double flower

A fuchsia flower before opening

A semi-double flower

A single flower

The flowers of the tender species *F. boliviana*

The flower of a triphylla-type fuchsia

four sepals that, before the flower opens, are joined together to form a characteristic, inverted teardrop-shaped structure. These split open, in many cases sweeping back (reflexing), to reveal the corolla, which comprises four or more petals, the thread-like organs known as the stamens and the central, longer style. If the corolla consists of only four petals, the flower is described as single (all species have single flowers). Those with eight petals are classified as double. Some flowers have five to seven petals and, strictly speaking, are defined as semi-double, but in practice these, too, are often loosely referred to as double.

A defining characteristic of the fuchsia is that the tube and sepals are colored (in most other plants they are green). If all the parts of the flower are the same color, it is described as self-colored (a self), but most fuchsias combine at least two colors, either contrasting or complementary. Fuchsias bred from *F. triphylla* (usually referred to as triphylla fuchsias or triphylla types) are easily identified by their elongated tubes. The flowers are usually borne in bunches (botanically called racemes) at the ends of stems, whereas other hybrid fuchsias usually carry their flowers singly.

Plant Catalog

In the following plant catalog, fuchsias are grouped as hardy or tender. Tender fuchsias are further subdivided into bedding and hanging basket types and species. The divisions have been devised for ease of use by the gardener and have no botanical significance. The heights and spreads are what the plants will achieve given normal cultivation.

Hardy fuchsias

Hardy fuchsias tolerate temperatures of 23°F or below and thus can be grown outdoors in cool climates, though in some areas they may need winter protection. Most can also be grown in containers. Some are suitable for growing in rock gardens. The group includes some species.

 ■ LEFT
'ARMY NURSE'

Hardy fuchsia introduced in 1947. The small, freely produced, semi-double flowers have blue-violet corollas and deep carmine-red sepals. Height 5 feet, spread 3 feet. 'Army Nurse' can also be grown in a container and is suitable for training as a standard.

■ ABOVE
'ALICE HOFFMAN'

Hardy fuchsia introduced in 1911. The semi-double flowers, borne in profusion, are small with white corollas with red veins and rose-pink sepals. The foliage is bronze-tinted. Height and spread 2½ feet. 'Alice Hoffman' is a compact plant, suitable for growing in a container.

■ RIGHT
'BARBARA'

Hardy fuchsia introduced in 1971. The single flowers have tangerine-pink corollas and pale pink sepals. Height 3–4 feet, spread 2 feet. 'Barbara' is a vigorous, upright plant that makes a good standard.

■ OPPOSITE RIGHT
'HAWKSHEAD'

Hardy fuchsia introduced in 1962. The small single flowers are white tinged with green. Height 2 feet, spread 1½ feet. 'Hawkshead' makes a vigorous, upright plant.

■ ABOVE
'BRUTUS'

Hardy fuchsia introduced in 1897. The abundant single flowers have rich dark purple corollas, lighter toward the base, and cerise-red sepals. Height and spread 3 feet. 'Brutus' is a vigorous cultivar that is suitable for growing in containers; it may also be trained as a standard.

■ RIGHT
'CHARMING'

Hardy fuchsia introduced by 1889. The single flowers have rose-purple corollas and red sepals. Height 3 feet, spread 2 feet. 'Charming' is one of the oldest cultivars still generally available.

■ TOP RIGHT
'GENII'

Hardy fuchsia introduced in 1951. The small single flowers, with rich violet-purple corollas and cerise-red sepals, are carried among light yellow-green leaves. Height 5 feet, spread 2½ feet. 'Genii,' an upright and bushy cultivar, makes a good standard; it is sometimes sold as 'Genie' or 'Jeane.'

■ RIGHT
'FLASH'

Hardy fuchsia introduced around 1930. The small, abundant single flowers have light magenta corollas and light magenta-red sepals. Height 5 feet or more, spread 1⅔ feet. 'Flash' makes a vigorous, stiffly upright plant.

■ RIGHT
'TOM THUMB'

Hardy fuchsia introduced in 1850. The small single flowers, carried in abundance, have mauve-purple corollas and carmine-red sepals. Height and spread 1⅔ feet. 'Tom Thumb,' a compact, bushy cultivar, is suitable for rock gardens and may also be trained as a miniature standard.

■ LEFT
'PROSPERITY'

Hardy fuchsia introduced in 1942. The double flowers, produced in abundance, have pale rose-pink corollas and crimson sepals. Height 5 feet, spread 3 feet. 'Prosperity' makes a strong, upright plant; it is suitable for training as a standard.

■ OPPOSITE
F. MAGELLANICA VAR. *GRACILIS*

Hardy species fuchsia, a variant of *F. magellanica* introduced in 1767. The small single flowers, which are borne in profusion among variegated leaves, have purple corollas and red sepals. Height and spread to 5 feet or possibly more. *F. magellanica* var. *gracilis* is more slender in leaf and flower than the true species; cuttings may be difficult to root.

Tender fuchsias

Tender fuchsias will not withstand frost and thus cannot be overwintered outdoors successfully in cool climates. The group includes half-hardy fuchsias that can withstand short periods at 32°F, and those that need a winter minimum of 23°F or above (defined here as frost tender). Tender fuchsias are all suitable for growing in containers.

Bedding types

These are usually upright plants that can be used for summer bedding in cool climates.

■ ABOVE RIGHT
'ALF THORNLEY'

Half-hardy bedding fuchsia introduced in 1971. The double flowers have white corollas and rose-pink sepals. Height and spread 3 feet. 'Alf Thornley' is an outstanding double.

■ RIGHT
'CAROLINE'

Half-hardy bedding fuchsia introduced in 1967. The large single flowers are bell-shaped and have cyclamen-purple corollas and creamy pink sepals. Height 3 feet, spread 2 feet. 'Caroline,' an upright plant, is an outstanding fuchsia.

■ BELOW
'CHANG'

Half-hardy bedding fuchsia introduced in 1946. The single flowers have brilliant orange corollas and orange-red sepals that are tipped with green. Height 3 feet, spread 2½ feet A vigorous plant of ungainly habit, 'Chang' is valued principally for its unusually colored flowers.

■ LEFT
'CELIA SMEDLEY'

Half-hardy bedding fuchsia introduced in 1970. The single flowers, freely produced, have vivid currant-red corollas and very pale pink tubes and sepals. Height to 5 feet, spread 3 feet. 'Celia Smedley' is a vigorous plant with an upright habit.

■ **LEFT**
'COTTON CANDY'

Half-hardy bedding fuchsia introduced in 1962. The double flowers have pale pink corollas and blush white sepals. Height 3 feet, spread 2 feet. 'Cotton Candy,' an upright plant, makes a good standard.

■ **BELOW**
'DIANE BROWN'

Half-hardy bedding fuchsia, introduced in 1990. The single flowers have pale pink corollas and pure white sepals. Height and spread 2 feet. 'Diane Brown' holds its flowers outward, an unusual feature.

■ ABOVE

'EDEN PRINCESS'

Half-hardy bedding fuchsia introduced in 1984. The single flowers have rich pinkish-purple corollas and reddish-pink sepals. Height and spread 3 feet or more. 'Eden Princess' makes an upright, bushy plant, notable for its gold-green foliage.

■ RIGHT

'GAY PARASOL'

Half-hardy bedding fuchsia introduced in 1979. The double flowers have dark red-purple corollas and sepals that are ivory-white overlaid with magenta. Height 3 feet, spread 1½ feet. 'Gay Parasol' has non-recurving sepals that open like a parasol, hence the name.

■ ABOVE LEFT
'GOLDEN EDEN LADY'

Half-hardy bedding fuchsia introduced in 1982. The single flowers have violet-blue corollas veined with red and reddish-pink sepals. The leaves are yellow-green. Height 3 feet, spread 2½ feet. 'Golden Eden Lady' makes a good standard; it is a relative of 'Eden Lady.'

■ ABOVE RIGHT
'GORDON THORLEY'

Half-hardy bedding fuchsia introduced in 1985. The freely produced single flowers have white corollas veined with rose-pink; the sepals are pink. Height 5 feet, spread 2½ feet. 'Gordon Thorley' has an excellent color combination.

■ RIGHT

'LORD LONSDALE'

Half-hardy bedding fuchsia. Its date of
introduction is uncertain. The single
flowers are of unique coloring: the
corollas are salmon-orange and the sepals
are apricot-pink tipped with green.
Height 5 feet, spread 3 feet. 'Lord
Lonsdale' also has distinctive foliage; the
leaves are curled and crinkled, particularly
in spring.

■ OPPOSITE LEFT

'JOY PATMORE'

Half-hardy bedding fuchsia introduced in
1961. The single flowers, produced in
abundance, have carmine-red corollas with
white bases and wax-white sepals. Height
5 feet, spread 3 feet. 'Joy Patmore' makes
a good standard.

■ LEFT
'MONTEREY'

Half-hardy bedding fuchsia of unknown date. The single flowers have orange corollas and salmon-orange sepals. Height and spread 3 feet. 'Monterey' is valued for its unusual colors.

■ LEFT
'PINK FANTASIA'

Half-hardy bedding fuchsia, introduced in 1989. The single flowers have dark purple corollas veined with pink and pink sepals. Height and spread 3 feet. 'Pink Fantasia' holds its flowers erect from the plant.

■ OPPOSITE
'ROYAL VELVET'

Half-hardy bedding fuchsia introduced in 1962. The large double flowers have luminous deep purple corollas and crimson sepals. Height 2½ feet, spread 3 feet. 'Royal Velvet' makes an exceptionally good standard.

■ OPPOSITE
'SNOWFIRE'

Half-hardy bedding fuchsia introduced in 1978. The double flowers have bright pink to coral-red corollas and white sepals. Height 3 feet, spread 2 feet. 'Snowfire' makes a good standard.

■ ABOVE LEFT
'SILVER DAWN'

Half-hardy bedding fuchsia introduced in 1983. The large double flowers have azure-violet corollas and white sepals. Height and spread 3 feet. A popular cultivar, 'Silver Dawn' is prized for its pastel colors.

■ ABOVE RIGHT
'TOM WOODS'

Half-hardy bedding fuchsia introduced in 1980. The single, freely produced flowers have blue-purple corollas that fade to magenta and white sepals. Height 1½ feet, spread 1 foot. 'Tom Woods' makes a compact plant.

■ RIGHT
'TING-A-LING'

Half-hardy bedding fuchsia introduced in 1959. The single white flowers, faintly tinged with pink, are produced in abundance. Height 2 feet, spread 1½ feet. 'Ting-a-ling,' a stiff, upright plant, is susceptible to botrytis under glass.

Hanging basket types

Fuchsias of a lax, trailing habit that are best grown in containers raised above ground level.

■ **BELOW LEFT**
'DARK EYES'

Half-hardy fuchsia, suitable for a hanging basket, introduced in 1958. The double flowers, carried in abundance, have deep, pure violet-blue corollas and deep red sepals. Height and spread 3 feet. Though the flowers are of medium size only, they are usually perfectly formed. 'Dark Eyes' makes a good standard and can also be used for bedding.

■ **BELOW RIGHT**
'FALLING STARS'

Half-hardy fuchsia, suitable for a hanging basket, introduced in 1941. The single flowers have turkey-red corollas and pale scarlet sepals. Height 1 foot, spread 4 feet. 'Falling Stars' can also be trained as a standard.

■ ABOVE
'ETERNAL FLAME'

Half-hardy fuchsia, suitable for a hanging basket, introduced in 1941. The semi-double flowers are uniquely colored: the corollas are dusky rose-pink streaked with salmon-pink at the base of the petals; the sepals are salmon-orange. Height 1½ feet, spread 3 feet. 'Eternal Flame,' which makes a lax plant, holds its flowers outward. It can also be used for bedding.

■ RIGHT
'FROSTED FLAME'

Half-hardy fuchsia, suitable for a hanging basket, introduced in 1975. The large, single, barrel-shaped flowers are freely produced and have bright flame-red corollas and white sepals that are flushed pink. Height 1 foot, spread 3 feet. 'Frosted Flame' has an unusually long flowering season.

■ **ABOVE LEFT**

'GRANDMA SINTON'

Half-hardy fuchsia, suitable for a
hanging basket, introduced in 1986. The
double flowers have very pale pink
corollas and shell-pink sepals. Height
3 feet, spread 1½ feet. 'Grandma Sinton,'
which is very free flowering for a double
fuchsia, makes an excellent weeping
standard.

■ **LEFT**

'IGLOO MAID'

Half-hardy fuchsia, suitable for a hanging
basket, introduced in 1972. The double
flowers have white corollas tinged with
pink and white sepals, and are borne amid
yellowish-green foliage. Height 3 feet,
spread 2 feet. 'Igloo Maid' makes an
upright plant initially but spreads as it
develops; it can be trained as a weeping
standard. It can also be used for bedding.

■ OPPOSITE LEFT

'HAZEL'

Half-hardy fuchsia, suitable for a hanging basket, introduced in 1985. The double flowers have violet to rose-pink corollas and rose-pink sepals. Height 4 feet, spread 2 feet. 'Hazel' makes an initially upright then lax plant that can also be used for bedding.

■ RIGHT

'MANTILLA'

Frost tender, triphylla-type fuchsia, suitable for a hanging basket, introduced in 1947. The single flowers are rich carmine-pink and are carried among leaves that are tinged with bronze. Height 6 inches, spread 2½ feet. 'Mantilla' is slow-growing and needs good cultivation.

Species

Tender fuchsias, which are generally grown for their botanical interest as well as their flowers, need greenhouse cultivation in cool climates. Few species are commonly grown.

■ LEFT

F. SPLENDENS

Half-hardy species fuchsia introduced to cultivation in 1832. The small flowers have orange-scarlet corollas and orange-red tubes, the sepals tipped with yellowish-green. Height to 6 feet, spread to 3 feet. *F. splendens* is a beautiful plant that flowers best when its growth is restricted in a container.

Buying fuchsias

Hardy fuchsias are sold as container-grown plants throughout the growing season. Tender fuchsias are usually available only from early spring to mid-summer – as rooted cuttings in modules early in the season and as plantlets, also in modules, from mid- to late spring. These are intended for use as bedding plants, but can be potted up and grown on individually in containers. Larger plants are available in pots, for use as bedding or container plants. Mature, flowering specimens are also available, and are planted directly into the garden like a bedding plant or into a container.

When buying fuchsias, look for healthy plants with sturdy stems and evenly spaced leaves; reject any that have yellowing leaves or that are growing lopsidedly. Check the undersides of the leaves in particular for any signs of pest infestation or disease (see Pests and diseases). Always read the plant label carefully, as this usually gives an indication of the plant's habit and final size.

Most garden centers sell only the most popular varieties; if you would like something more unusual, go to a specialty grower. Most sell by mail order if there isn't one in your area. The plants are usually dispatched as small, module-grown plantlets, and should be potted up as soon as you receive them.

■ BELOW
Commercial growers who supply by mail order generally dispatch the plants in lightweight but highly protective packages.

Cultivation of hardy fuchsias

Hardy fuchsias should be planted in a position that is sheltered from hot sun in summer, but not beneath deciduous trees, where the plants will be heavily shaded by the time they flower in late summer. Variegated and yellow-leaved forms need some sun to enhance the leaf color, but full sun can cause leaf scorching in summer.

They tolerate a wide range of conditions but generally prefer a neutral to slightly acid, moderately fertile soil – over-rich soil can lead to excessive leafy growth at the expense of flowers. You can test whether your soil is acid or alkaline with a soil-testing kit, available at most garden centers.

To determine your soil texture, squeeze a small amount of moist soil in your hand. If it fails to hold together and slips through your fingers, your soil is sandy. Such soils are easy to work and warm up quickly in spring, but lose fertility easily as nutrients tend to percolate through them. A solid lump that retains the imprint of your hand indicates a clay soil. These are wet, heavy and slow to warm up, but retain nutrients well. The ideal for fuchsias is a soil that will form crumbs and leave your hands clean as you rub it through your fingers.

A massed planting of fuchsias that includes both hardy and tender types.

To improve your soil, work in organic matter: farmyard manure, old mushroom compost or garden compost. It helps to retain moisture in dry, sandy soils and opens up the texture of heavy soils, allowing water to drain more freely. Drainage can also be improved by digging in a bucketful of grit per square yard. Make sure that any manure is well rotted, or it will take nitrogen from the soil as it decomposes; mushroom compost tends to be alkaline – use only on soils that are neutral to acid.

Planting hardy fuchsias

Hardy fuchsias are best planted in mid- to late spring, after the last frosts in cold climates. Large plants establish faster than small ones; if a plant is little more than a rooted cutting, transplant it into a larger pot

The following fuchsias will survive several degrees of frost in gardens:

'Alice Hoffman'

x *bacillaris*

'Brutus'

'Chillerton Beauty'

'Display'

'Dollar Princess'

'Flash'

'Garden News'

'Genii'

'Lady Thumb'

'Lena'

'Madame Cornelissen'

magellanica and forms

'Margaret'

'Mrs Popple'

'Phyllis'

'Pixie'

'Prosperity'

'Riccartonii'

'Rose of Castile'

'Temple Bells'

'Tom Thumb'

'Trase'

1 First, fork over the site to break up the soil, and remove any weeds. Then dig a hole roughly twice the depth and twice the diameter of the pot.

2 Establish the planting depth by laying a cane across the hole. You should aim to cover the base of the stems up to one or two leaf joints.

3 Backfill so the soil surface is level with the surrounding soil. Firm in with your fingers.

4 Water in well, then apply a mulch of garden compost or well-rotted farmyard manure around the base of the plant to reduce water evaporation.

and grow it for 6–8 weeks before planting it out (see Potting on).

Deep planting is recommended in frost-prone areas, since this encourages the production of fresh shoots from below ground level each spring. You need to ensure that the lowest one or two buds are below soil level.

For a hedge, prepare a trench about 1 foot wide and deep and fork organic matter into the base.

The following fuchsias are suitable for growing as hedges:

magellanica and forms

'Mrs Popple'

'Phyllis'

Set the plants about 1½ feet apart; in an exposed site, where the plants will not grow so large, reduce the planting distance to 1 foot. For a dense hedge, stagger the fuchsias in a zigzag. Use plants of one variety only, to ensure uniform growth.

You will need to water the plants regularly during their first season, particularly during dry spells. Thereafter, provided you apply a deep mulch in spring, watering during the rest of the growing season should not be necessary.

Once established, hardy fuchsias need little attention, apart from annual pruning (see Pruning a hardy fuchsia) and a mulch of organic matter in spring to help maintain soil fertility, improve soil structure and retain moisture.

In cold areas, mulch in winter with a dry material such as salt hay, dried leaves or straw, to protect the crowns.

■ LEFT

For extra protection in cold climates, cover the crowns of hardy fuchsias with a dry mulch in winter.

Planting bedding fuchsias

Bedding fuchsias are usually sold as plantlets in modules. For the best display you need to plant them early in the season to allow them to develop fully. If you cannot plant until late spring or early summer, because late frosts are frequent, either pot up the plantlets and grow them on under glass (see Overwintering and cultivation under glass) or buy pot-grown plants later on. If you are worried by the threat of a late frost after planting, protect the plants with cloches, or cover the whole row with air- and water-permeable horticultural fleece or an old net curtain. Hold down the edges with bricks to prevent it from blowing away.

Fuchsias particularly recommended for bedding:

'Estelle Marie'

'Koralle'

'Margaret Roe'

'Nellie Nuttall'

'Thalia'

For the best results, restrict yourself to one variety of fuchsia. Mixed cultivars will grow at different rates, and the overall effect will be "spotty." Whichever type you choose, you should prepare the bed in advance, but do not incorporate organic matter, for too rich a soil will lead to excessive leafy growth at the expense of flowers. Bedding fuchsias tolerate a position in full sun provided the soil does not dry out completely in summer. You can sink container-grown fuchsias directly into the soil in their pots. This may even accelerate and improve flowering, since the roots are restricted, but you will need to water and feed more frequently during the summer.

After flowering, either lift the old plants and discard them, or pot them up and overwinter them for use next year (see Overwintering and cultivation under glass). Alternatively, take cuttings to maintain your stock (see Propagation).

1 Fork over the site to break up the soil; remove any weeds, using a hand fork, and rake over the soil to level it.

2 Use a straight edge to mark the positions of the plants. Space them evenly from 8 inches to 1¼ feet. Check their ultimate size – at their peak, they should touch, but not restrict each other's growth.

3 Plant the fuchsias and pat them in with your fingers.

■ LEFT
A rich planting of bedding fuchsias flanked by *Dahlia* 'Bishop of Llandaff' and backed by a yew hedge.

4 Water well. Once planted, water the fuchsias frequently, particularly in times of drought, and feed as for potted plants (see Growing in containers).

5 If a late frost threatens, protect the plants with a cloche. The top half of a clear plastic soda bottle, with the cap removed to allow for air circulation, makes a good improvised cloche for small plants.

Growing in containers

Few plants lend themselves to pot cultivation so readily as fuchsias. Choice of soil mix is a personal matter. Soil-based mixtures are likely to be more expensive and heavy, so you may prefer peat-based types that are lighter. These, however, have the disadvantage of being difficult to re-wet if you allow them to dry out, so frequent watering is essential. Conversely, they also retain moisture, which can lead to waterlogging if you water too generously, though working a little perlite, vermiculite or horticultural grit into the mixture will help drainage. Grow mixes based on renewable resources such as coir have properties similar to peat-based grow mixes.

Fuchsias in containers need regular watering and feeding. To test whether the plants need watering, press your finger into the soil mix at the edge of the pot. If the soil mix feels cool and moist, watering is unnecessary. You will need to water at least once and probably twice a day at the height of summer.

It is good practice to start feeding immediately after planting. The proportions of chemicals in proprietary fertilizers are listed on the label. Those referred to as "straights," or described as "balanced," contain equal amounts of the major elements: nitrogen (N), phosphorus (P) and potassium (K). You will have good results by using one of these exclusively throughout the season. For optimum performance, however, use a high nitrogen fertilizer during the first two months of growth, pot on regularly (see opposite) and pinch prune (see Pruning), then switch to a high-potassium fertilizer as flowerbuds begin to appear. The plants take up the nutrients most readily if the fertilizer is applied as a foliar feed.

Potting on

To develop a large, floriferous plant, you need to repot it into increasingly larger pots, a practice known as potting on. This keeps the roots growing actively and inhibits flower production: the plant's energies are channeled into producing leafy growth, particularly if you apply a nitrogen-high fertilizer regularly.

You can pot on whenever the fuchsia's roots fill the pot. You can easily test for this by watering the plant well, letting it drain, then sliding it out of its pot. If the surface of the soil mix is "netted" with roots, it is safe to repot the plant. How regularly you pot on depends on how quickly the plant grows. By continuing to pot on, you can delay the onset of flowering virtually indefinitely, provided you also feed with a high nitrogen fertilizer and shorten the growing points regularly (see Pruning).

When potting on, always pot into the next size pot: potting into too large a pot too soon may upset the plant's growth rate. Follow the steps shown here when potting up module-grown plantlets also. When you have produced a large, healthy plant, pot it into its final container for flower production (see Planting a decorative container).

1 The roots of this fuchsia have filled the pot so it should now be potted on.

2 Line the base of the new pot with crocks or small stones to cover the drainage holes. Cover with a thin layer of soil mix.

3 Place the plant in the center of the pot and fill the gap around the edge with fresh soil mix.

Repotting

When new growth starts to emerge on overwintered plants (see Overwintering and cultivation under glass), you need to replace some or all of the old soil mix, since its nutrients will have been exhausted. When repotting, always return the plant to the same pot or to another pot of the same size. This is a good opportunity to check for the presence of vine weevil larvae that attack the roots of the plant (see Pests and diseases). Trimming the root system helps to stimulate the growth of new feeding roots. These will readily take up the fresh nutrients available and thus new top-growth is accelerated.

In the case of large fuchsias that have reached their full size and established standards, you may find it easier to top-dress than repot, i.e. to replace the top few inches of soil mix. Both repotting and top-dressing are easiest if the soil mix in the pot is dry.

1 To repot, make sure the old soil mix is dry, cradle the lower stems of the plant in your hand, and ease it out of its pot.

2 Carefully shake the roots free of the old soil mix.

3 Lightly trim over the roots with pruners. Line the base of the pot with fresh soil mix and return the plant.

4 Fill the pot with soil mix, shaking it gently to settle the soil mix around the roots. Then water to settle the plant in the pot.

TOP-DRESSING

1 To top-dress, with the plant held at an angle, scrape away the top layer of old soil mix to expose some of the roots. The soil mix should be dry.

2 Fill in with fresh soil mix, then water as in step 4 (above).

Planting a decorative container

From mid-summer onwards, sometimes earlier, mature, flowering fuchsias are available at garden centers. Since the nutrient content of the soil mix will probably be exhausted, to get the best out of them, you need to pot them up immediately.

Use a proprietary potting soil mix (see Growing in containers). If you need to reduce the overall weight of the planted container, instead of covering the base with broken china or stones, substitute broken pieces of styrofoam and lighten the soil mix by replacing up to a third of it with perlite or vermiculite. As these are inert, you will need to feed more often to compensate. Conversely, if you need to add weight, mix in some horticultural grit.

■ RIGHT
Planted directly into a decorative container, a mature, flowering fuchsia makes an instant impact. To keep it at its peak, feed and water well until the first frosts.

Keep the containers well-watered, particularly during dry spells. The use of water-retaining gel in step 2 can help prevent the soil mix from drying out between waterings. Feed regularly with a high potassium feed to keep the plant flowering profusely throughout the summer.

1 Cover the base holes with broken china or pieces of styrofoam.

2 Fill the base of the pot with a layer of soil mix. Add the fuchsia; there must be a ¾-inch gap between the soil surface and rim of the pot for watering. Add water-retaining gel, if required.

3 Remove the fuchsia from its pot, place in the center of the soil mix and fill in with more soil mix.

4 Water well to help settle the plant.

Planting a hanging basket

Any of the trailing fuchsia varieties make an ideal subject for a hanging basket: here, we used 'La Campanella' with variegated ivies, trailing blue and white lobelias, and a variegated *Sedum*. Remember to use multiples of the same fuchsia variety, since different varieties may flower at different times. For the best display, use as many plants as you can fit into the basket, then feed and water copiously as they grow. At the height of summer, you will need to water at least once and probably twice a day.

It is best to use a soil-less grow mix for a hanging basket, since it is lighter than soil-based types. To lessen the danger of the grow mix drying out between waterings, add a water-retaining gel as you fill the basket. Plant the basket when all danger of frost has passed. If you have a greenhouse or conservatory that is frost free, however, you can plant

The following fuchsias are suitable for growing in hanging baskets:

'Autumnale'

x *bacillaris*

'Cascade'

'Flying Cloud'

'Golden Marinka'

'Golden Swingtime'

'Harry Gray'

'Hula Girl'

'Jack Shahan'

'La Campanella'

'Marinka'

'Mrs. W Rundle'

'Orange Drops'

'Pink Galore'

procumbens

'Red Spider'

'Strawberry Delight'

'Swingtime'

'Texas Longhorn'

'Westminster Chimes'

'White Spider'

earlier in the year. This will give it a head start, and earlier flowers. Site the basket so it is in shade at midday.

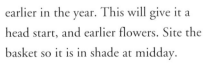

■ LEFT
To keep a basket flowering well throughout the summer, use a high-potassium liquid fertilizer every 7–10 days.

1 Position the basket on a flat surface, or place it over a pot to steady it. Line the basket with a hanging basket liner of the appropriate size.

2 Cut a disc of plastic to fit the base of the basket. This stops water from draining through the basket too quickly.

3 Fill the basket approximately half full with grow mix. Add some water-retaining gel, following the manufacturer's instructions, and fork it in.

4 Using scissors or a knife, cut holes in the side of the liner for the trailing plants to hang through.

5 Carefully, push the plants through the liner.

6 Continue to add grow mix and more trailing plants, then position the central plant, in this case 'La Campanella.'

7 Add slow-release fertilizer; the pelleted type is easiest to use.

8 Add more trailing plants around the side. Slope the root balls so the heads of the plants trail down around the edge of the basket. Add more grow mix to level the top.

9 Stand the basket on top of a large pot, then water it thoroughly to settle the plants in. Let it drain before hanging up.

Overwintering and cultivation under glass

Overwintering

Gardeners in cold climates can easily bring tender fuchsias through the winter and enjoy them again the following year, but if you do not have a heated greenhouse you need to induce a period of dormancy. Toward the end of the season, stand the plants for a few weeks in a position where they will receive maximum sun. Any plant that has been grown in a container, either sunk in the ground or as a patio plant, can be left in its pot. To preserve bedding plants, lift them after flowering, shake the roots free of soil and pot them up (see Repotting). The leaves may shrivel and drop off in the sun, but the heat will ripen the stems, and help them to withstand low temperatures. Before the first frosts, transfer the plants to a light, cool but frost-free environment such as a spare bedroom or a porch. Water only to prevent the soil mix from drying out completely, and do not feed until the following spring.

Cultivation under glass

To grow tender fuchsias successfully under glass, you need to monitor temperature, humidity and light levels closely.

Small greenhouses heat up much more rapidly than large ones, and high temperatures are detrimental to fuchsias. Furthermore, cramming too many plants into too small a space can adversely affect the plants' growth and increase their susceptibility to disease and attacks from pests (see Pests and diseases).

In spring and summer, while the plants are in active growth, watch the temperature carefully. A maximum-minimum thermometer is essential. Once the daytime temperature in the greenhouse begins to rise above 50°F, you need to ventilate, using automatic vent openers that are heat-sensitive, if necessary.

When the temperature rises above 75°F you need to create shade, both to cut the light level and reduce heat. You can either apply a wash to the outside of the glass, use slatted wooden blinds on the outside that can be rolled up or down, or use

OVERWINTERING TENDER FUCHSIAS

1 Lift each plant with a fork and shake the roots free of soil.

2 Pot up plants individually, using a soil- or peat-based grow mix.

3 Cut the top growth back lightly and remove any dead leaves.

■ LEFT
A wash applied to the outside of the glass prevents the greenhouse from overheating in summer.

In winter, you need to provide maximum light. Remove all shading. You can keep the greenhouse frost free in a variety of ways. Electric and gas heaters are clean to run and can be thermostatically controlled. In any event they need frequent checkups to be certain all remains in order. When any heater is used, you also need to ventilate, since any fumes could be toxic to plants.

A winter minimum of a couple of degrees above freezing is sufficient to ensure the survival of your plants, but taller standards require slightly higher winter temperatures to keep the plants semi-dormant in order to produce a large flowering head in proportion to the stem the following season. A temperature of 41–55°F. will keep the plants green and may even maintain growth. This temperature is also necessary for the successful overwintering of triphylla types. They will survive if allowed to become dormant at lower temperatures, but fresh growth the following spring is usually slow to emerge.

The following spring, as the overwintered plants begin to grow, or growth accelerates, top-dress or repot them (see Repotting).

green plastic woven mesh on the inside or outside of the greenhouse. Colored bubble-plastic is unsuitable: it cuts down light without reducing the temperature significantly.

At night during summer, a drop to 65°F or lower is essential for flower bud initiation; if the temperature in the greenhouse remains high at night, either move the plants outdoors or install a thermostatically controlled air-cooling system.

Hose down the floor daily in the morning during hot weather to maintain humidity (at the height of summer, repeat in the evenings) and mist the plants. Use ordinary tap water, but if you live in an area with very hard water, mist with clean rainwater collected in a water barrel.

Propagation

One of the pleasures of growing fuchsias is the ease with which new plants can be raised from cuttings. They can be taken at any time of year when the plants are in active growth. Cuttings taken just as the plants are coming into growth in early spring will root, grow and flower the same year – the earlier in the season you take the cutting, the faster it is to root, but those taken very early need bottom heat, around 65–70°F in a heated propagator. Always use material from strong, vigorous shoots on healthy specimens.

The cuttings grow mix should be inert (i.e. contain no nutrients that might encourage leaf growth rather than root development). Use a mixture of equal parts peat substitute and perlite, or any other infertile materials such as vermiculite or horticultural grit or sand. Hormone rooting compounds are not necessary.

Keep the cuttings in a closed case to maintain humidity and place in shade to prevent overheating. The humidity will keep the cuttings firm and encourage rooting. A reasonably sterile environment is essential while the roots are forming, or fungal growths may occur. Feed the cuttings once roots have formed.

1 Using a sharp, clean knife, remove a section about 2–3 inches long from the end of a non-flowering shoot, cutting just above a leaf joint.

2 Trim the cutting below the lowest set of leaves.

3 Then remove the lower leaves from the stem.

4 Dip the cutting in a copper-based fungicide solution to sterilize them.

5 Fill a 3-inch pot with cuttings grow mix, water it and let drain. Make holes with a dibber and insert the cuttings. Pat them in with your fingers.

■ LEFT
The cuttings
should root within
6 weeks. Pot them
up individually,
label, and grow
them on.

6 Spray the cuttings with the fungicide solution.

7 Make sure the cuttings do not touch the sides of the propagating unit because this may cause moisture to build up, leading to rotting. Label the cuttings and place them in a closed case.

8 Regularly wipe down the condensation that forms on the inside of the case with a cloth or a piece of paper towel, wrung out in an antiseptic solution.

Pruning

Most pruning procedures are straight-forward, provided you bear a few basic principles in mind. Remember that pruning always stimulates fresh, vigorous growth from a point near to the cut. Cut a bare stem and you will get new growth only from near the cut, while the bottom part of the stem stays bare. If you cut a vigorous stem back hard, it will grow back with redoubled vigor, so prune these only lightly, if at all. Conversely, hard pruning encourages weak shoots to grow strongly. Fuchsias are quick-growing and you will see the results of your actions after a very short time.

When carrying out any pruning, use pruners that have clean, sharp blades. Blunt tools will not cut cleanly and will snag the wood, providing an entry point for disease. Clean the blades after use and keep them well oiled.

Pruning a hardy fuchsia

Since fuchsias flower on the current season's growth, prune in spring as the new growth begins. Delay, and you run the risk of losing that season's flowers. Where winters are mild and the plants remain green, pruning can be restricted to the removal of any dead, diseased or damaged wood, but you can also shorten stems by about one-third in early spring for more compact growth. On hedges, shorten the laterals (side shoots) by up to half. Shortening all the current season's growth by around one-third after flowering in autumn will make

PRUNING A HARDY FUCHSIA

1 In spring, new growth emerges from the crown of the plant, pushing through any winter mulch that remains.

2 Cut the dead stems back hard, as near to ground level as possible.

3 After pruning, the plant has more access to the light and will grow strongly. Leave any remaining mulch in place; it will gradually break down and improve the soil structure.

the plant less prone to wind damage.

In frost-prone situations, pruning is really a matter of renovation, since all the previous year's growth will usually be dead and has to be cut away. As the days begin to lengthen and hard frosts become less frequent, you need to make room for the new shoots emerging from the base of the plant.

Pruning a tender fuchsia

Tender fuchsias have varying pruning needs. Species, in general, require no pruning at all, though if you grow them as potted plants under glass you can restrict their spread by shortening the stems by between one-third and a half in spring. Hybrids should be pruned regularly. Since they have soft stems, most pruning is best carried out with finger and thumb, a technique known as pinch pruning or stopping.

Pinch pruning

The aim of pinch pruning is to develop a compact plant that will flower over its entire surface. By removing the ends of stems, the

■ LEFT
Annual pruning
has kept this
specimen of *F.
magellanica* var.
molinae healthy,
vigorous and free-
flowering.

PINCH PRUNING

With finger and thumb, or with a sharp
razor blade or scissors, shorten stems to
two or three sets of leaves.

DEAD-HEADING

Pinch out dead and fading flowers close to
the leaf joint.

PRUNING AN OVERWINTERED TENDER FUCHSIA

1 By spring, the fuchsia will probably
have lost almost all of the previous
year's leaves.

2 Cut back the previous year's stems by
as much as two-thirds, cutting just
above a point where new shoots can be
seen to emerge. Remove any thin,
unproductive stems entirely, then repot or
top-dress, water well, and feed.

Deciding how often to prune and
how rigorously depends on taste and
the plant's natural habit. A strict
regime applied to a vigorous, bushy
plant will result in a very formal,
almost geometric, dome-shaped
specimen (for a really compact plant,
you can even pinch prune after each
set of leaves). Lax-growing, hanging
basket types develop their most
elegant habit if pinch pruned only in
the early stages of growth.

Dead-heading

Removing fading flowers not only
improves the appearance of the plant,
but also prolongs the flowering season
by encouraging the production of a
further flush of flowers. By
consistently taking off the old flowers,
you ensure that your fuchsias will
bloom until the first frost.

Pruning an overwintered tender fuchsia

To bring overwintered tender
fuchsias back into active growth,
prune as shown above left, water well,
repot or top-dress (see Repotting),
then boost with a high-nitrogen feed.
Spraying the old wood with water
also helps the dormant buds to break.

plant's energies are diverted into dormant side buds in the leaf axils (the
point where a leaf joins the stem).
Where the leaves are in pairs, two
new shoots will develop; where they
are in threes, three new shoots arise.

Once these new shoots have grown
three or more sets of leaves, they too
can be pinch pruned. In general, you
need to stop pinch pruning around
early to mid-summer, and the flowers
will develop six to eight weeks later.

Training

Training a standard

Growing fuchsias as standards is perhaps the most rewarding way of treating these plants. Though the results are spectacular, the technique involved is very simple, and you can train a standard to any height up to about 5 feet. By choosing vigorous subjects and starting training early – say in early spring – it is theoretically possible to produce a flower-bearing standard within the space of a single growing season. For really quick results, apply a high-nitrogen feed during the first two months of training and pot on regularly (see Potting on) until you begin to develop the head of the standard. You will produce stronger plants with larger heads, however, by allowing them to develop without flowering during the first year, then keeping them semi-dormant during the winter (see Overwintering). At the start of the second growing season, as new shoots emerge, trim over the head to create a balanced shape, cutting stems back by about a quarter to one-third. If any shoots arise lower down on the main stem, rub them out with finger and thumb.

Less vigorous cultivars can also be trained as standards and produce equally good results, but take longer to develop.

■ LEFT
A trailing fuchsia trained as a weeping standard.

TRAINING A STANDARD

1 Choose a healthy, vigorous, well-rooted, single-stemmed cutting, preferably with leaves in threes.

2 Pot the cutting into a 3-inch pot and insert a cane next to the stem. Tie the stem firmly to the cane with a wire tie, but allow room for the stem to thicken as it grows; otherwise the stem may develop a kink at that point.

3 *(left)* As the stem develops, remove side shoots that form in the leaf axils, apart from the top two or three at the tip of the main stem. Leave the large leaves on the main stem intact; these help to feed the plant and will eventually drop off naturally. Continue to tie the stem to the cane.

4 Once the stem has reached the desired height, pinch out the growing tip. This will encourage the side shoots remaining in the upper leaf axils to develop, and they will form the head.

5 As the side shoots grow, continue pinching out the tips of each shoot after every two or three leaves.

The following fuchsias are suitable for growing as standards:

'Annabel'
'Army Nurse'
'Celia Smedley'
'Checkerboard'
'Cloverdale Pearl'
'Dark Eyes'
'Eden Lady'
'Garden News'
'Genii'
'Golden Dawn'
'Golden Swingtime'
'Heidi Ann'
'Joy Patmore'
'Lady Thumb' (miniature)
'Lena'
'Margaret'
'Marin Glow'
'Mrs W Rundle'
'Nellie Nuttall'
'Pacquesa'
'Peppermint Stick'
'Rose of Castile'
'Royal Velvet'
'Rufus'
'Snowcap'
'Strawberry Delight'
'Swingtime'
'Tennessee Waltz'
'Texas Longhorn'
'Tom Thumb' (miniature)
'Tristesse'
'White Ann'
'White Spider'

A standard fuchsia in a container makes a striking focal point.

of stems near the base of the plant: if you try to create the shape using just a few long shoots, they may shed their leaves near the base as they grow.

In frost-free climates, you can also train fuchsias as fans outdoors against a wall. Fix a framework of canes in a fan shape to the wall. Prepare the ground and plant as for a hardy fuchsia, positioning the fuchsia at least 1 foot from the wall and angling the stems toward it. Tie these in to the canes as they grow.

Pinch out the leading shoot of a bushy, vigorous cultivar and allow the laterals to develop two or three sets of leaves. Insert canes in the soil mix in a fan shape and attach suitably placed laterals to them with wire ties. Continue to tie them in as they grow.

Training a fan

Training fuchsias as fans is one of the simplest decorative effects, provided you choose a bushy, vigorous cultivar that is growing evenly. Repotting is impractical, however, once the framework of canes is in place, so you will need to feed the plant regularly as it develops. Choose a young specimen of a bushy cultivar. Shorten the leading shoot (the upright shoot that grows in the center of the plant) to encourage the side shoots to lengthen. You need to pinch prune regularly early on (see Pruning) to ensure a lot

Pests and diseases

Generally speaking, fuchsias are trouble-free, particularly those grown in the open garden in conjunction with other plants that attract beneficial insects as well as pests. Under glass, however, you may encounter problems, as the conditions that fuchsias need are exactly the same as those many pests also enjoy. Problems will be worsened if you grow a lot of fuchsias in close proximity, since they will all attract the same pests, and these will rapidly multiply and form a dominant population. Prevention is better than cure, however, and if you keep the plants healthy and growing strongly, feeding and watering them as necessary, no attack need result in heavy losses.

Maintain good hygiene at all times. In spring each year, empty the greenhouse of all plants. Clean the windows with plain water, ideally applied with a pressure-washer if they are very dirty. Wash down the floor and any staging with a horticultural disinfectant. When returning the plants to the greenhouse, space them well apart, to prevent them from growing lopsidedly, and to ensure good air circulation. If you buy new plants, keep them apart from your main stock for a couple of weeks until

you are satisfied that the newcomers are disease-free.

Check your plants regularly for any signs of pests and diseases and routinely remove any dead leaves or flowers that may encourage molds or provide nesting places for pests. If you do spot a diseased or damaged plant, isolate it and treat both it and any others that show the same symptoms, then treat those plants as yet unaffected. Seriously damaged plants should be discarded.

Fortunately, the two pests you are most likely to encounter, whitefly and red spider mite, are easily controlled with chemical sprays or fumigants (insecticidal smokes), though some strains are best controlled biologically. If you use a spray, remember to treat the undersides of the leaves as well as the surfaces. When using any insecticide, follow the manufacturer's instructions and take any precautions necessary; wear a protective mask or gloves when their use is recommended.

All the problems described relate to fuchsias being grown under glass. When practical, it is always a good idea to move plants outdoors during the summer months, where it is generally cooler; air

circulation is better and there are higher numbers of beneficial insects.

Aphid

How to identify: Tiny green insects that are also found on plants outdoors, especially roses (greenfly). You are most likely to identify them by the damage they cause, however: leaves are sticky and may curl

Aphid

at the edges and black sooty molds may take hold. Plants that are not too seriously affected may recover, but the moldy patches may provide an entry point for viruses.
Cause: Failure to spray regularly. Since these pests thrive in the environment that is most beneficial to fuchsias, they are likely to proliferate unless preventative action is taken.
Control: Spray with an insecticide or use a fumigant.
Prevention: Treat the plants regularly from the onset of the growing season. During the

summer, moving them outdoors will lessen the likelihood of attack, as more predators will be present in the garden environment.

Botrytis

How to identify: A fuzzy, gray mold, that can be seen on any part of the top growth of the plant, but most commonly on the stems and

Botrytis

leaves.
Cause: Too high a humidity at too low a temperature. The problem is most likely to occur in winter and spring.
Control: Remove and discard all affected growth. Spray with a fungicide or use a horticultural smoke.
Prevention: Check humidity and temperature levels regularly, particularly when the temperature outdoors is low. Make sure your plants are not crowded together and also that air can freely circulate.

Red spider mite

How to identify: Leaves become transparent and papery as the mites eat the undersides. They turn yellow, then brown, before dropping off. The mites themselves, however, are tiny, so you are unlikely to spot them until they have multiplied and cluster together.
Cause: Hot, dry conditions

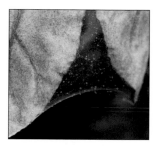

Red spider mite

that encourage the pest to breed.
Control: Some strains have developed a resistance to conventional pesticides, so introduce the predatory mite *Phytoseiulus persimilis,* usually available by mail order.
Prevention: Keep the greenhouse well ventilated during hot weather, shade the plants and water down the floor at least twice a day. Misting the plants occasionally (wetting the undersides of the leaves also) additionally helps to deter the red spider mites.

Rust

How to identify: An orange powdery deposit (fungal spores), later turning brown, on the undersides of leaves; corresponding black or yellow spots appear on the upper surfaces. The leaves may drop off.
Cause: High humidity; the spores are spread on air currents and in water droplets. Most infestations arise

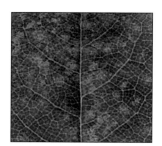

Rust

from newly bought plants that are already affected.
Control: Remove and burn all affected leaves. Also burn any seriously damaged plants. Spray the remainder with a fungicide at regular intervals.
Prevention: Difficult, but keeping the plants away from open doors and windows may help. Watering and spraying plants individually will prevent the possible transfer of spores from one plant to another. When buying new plants, quarantine them for a few weeks until you are certain they are disease-free.

Vine weevil and its larvae

How to identify: Growth is slow or stops altogether. The damage is caused by the larvae of a flightless beetle that lays its eggs on the surface of the soil mix. The adult beetles eat leaves, but established plants will recover. Worse damage is caused by the creamy white larvae that, in winter and

Vine weevil and its larvae

early spring, attack the roots of plants and thus are seldom seen. You may, however, notice the grubs when repotting in spring.
Cause: Failure to eradicate the parent beetle before it lays its eggs in late spring and early summer.
Control: Spray with insecticide whenever the pests are active. To eradicate the larvae, use an insecticidal root drench in mid-summer. Older larvae are resistant to the chemical controls available, however; to eradicate these, introduce parasitic nematodes into the

soil mix in late summer.
Prevention: Maintain good hygiene and systematically remove fallen leaves that may provide hiding places for the adult beetles.

Whitefly

How to identify: Tiny white moth-like insects; their eggs are found on the undersides of leaves from late spring. The

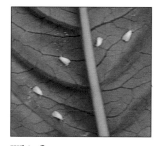

Whitefly

upper surfaces may be covered in a sticky deposit that eventually attracts sooty molds.
Cause: High temperatures that encourage the pests to breed.
Control: From spring, spray with a soap-based insecticide or use a fumigant. Regular applications over a period of several weeks may be necessary. Alternatively, introduce the parasitic wasp *Encarsia formosa,* available by mail order.
Prevention: Maintain the appropriate temperature.

Calendar

EARLY SPRING

Hardy

In cold climates, cut back hardy fuchsias to ground level. Trim lateral branches on hedges by around a half. Fertilize and mulch after pruning.

Tender

Prune hybrid fuchsias kept dormant over winter. Pot them on, top-dress or repot. Trim the roots as necessary and check for vine weevil larvae. Mist the top growth to encourage dormant buds to break and feed the plants with a high-nitrogen fertilizer. Empty greenhouses of all plants. Clean the windows with water and wash the floor and any staging with a horticultural disinfectant. Trim back the top growth of tender species in containers, overwintered in a heated greenhouse. Outdoors, prepare the ground for bedding fuchsias.

MID- TO LATE SPRING

Hardy

Plant new stock, after the last severe frost in cold climates.

Tender

Pinch prune to encourage bushiness. Begin to train new standards and continue to pinch out the side shoots of one-year-old, overwintered standards. Water and feed all fuchsias in containers regularly. Take cuttings to increase your stock. Pot on cuttings taken the previous year. In greenhouses, check the humidity level regularly and watch out for renewed pest activity. Maintain good greenhouse hygiene.

Outdoors, plant out bedding fuchsias, after the last hard frost. Protect them with cloches if frosts are a threat. Plant baskets; move them under cover if frost is a threat.

EARLY TO MID-SUMMER

Hardy

Take cuttings to increase your stock.

Tender

Stop pinch pruning and feed with a high-potassium fertilizer to promote better flowering. Continue to pinch prune specimens whose flowering you wish to delay. Take cuttings and pot on any cuttings struck in spring. Water fuchsias in containers freely. Remove all flowers as they fade. In greenhouses, keep a careful watch for any sign of pest infestation and

Pale pink 'Harry Gray' in a container lights up a shady corner.

disease attacks. Check the humidity and temperature levels. Maintain good greenhouse hygiene.

LATE SUMMER

Hardy

Take cuttings to increase your stock.

Tender

Take cuttings to increase your stock. Lift and pot up bedding plants for overwintering. Stand them and all other fuchsias in containers in a warm, sunny spot; this will soon ripen the wood. Gradually cut down on the amount of watering and do not feed. In greenhouses, continue to look out for any sign of pest and disease attacks and maintain good greenhouse hygiene.

AUTUMN-WINTER

Hardy

Cover the crowns of hardy fuchsias with a dry mulch as the leaves begin to wither and fall. In exposed sites, trim back hedges by about one-third to make the plants more compact and to minimize wind-rock.

Tender

Bring all fuchsias that have spent the summer outdoors into a cool, light, frost-free environment. Water occasionally to prevent the soil mix from drying out completely, but do not fertilize. In greenhouses that are heated to keep the plants in active growth, remove all shading and check the humidity level regularly.

Other recommended fuchsias

'**Annabel**' Half-hardy bedding fuchsia. Double flowers have white corollas veined with pink-and-white sepals flushed with pink. A good standard.
'**Autumnale**' Half-hardy fuchsia suitable for a hanging basket. Single flowers have purple corollas and red sepals.

Grown mainly for its large golden leaves flushed with bronze.
x *bacillaris* Hardy fuchsia. Tiny flowers are white, pink or red. Grow in a rock garden or hanging basket.
'**Cascade**' Half-hardy fuchsia suitable for a hanging basket.

Single flowers have deep carmine-red sepals and white sepals flushed with carmine-red. Free-flowering.
'**Celia Smedley**' Half-hardy bedding fuchsia. Single flowers have vivid currant-red corollas and pale rose-pink sepals. Free-flowering.

'**Checkerboard**' Half-hardy bedding fuchsia. Single flowers have deep red corollas and red sepals that turn abruptly white. A good standard.
'**Chillerton Beauty**' Hardy fuchsia. Single flowers have mauve-violet corollas and pale rose-pink sepals. Free-flowering.
'**Cloverdale Pearl**' Half-hardy bedding fuchsia. Single flowers have white corollas and pale pink sepals. A good standard.
'**Display**' Hardy fuchsia. Single flowers have deep cerise-pink corollas and rose-pink sepals. A good standard.
'**Dollar Princess**' Hardy fuchsia. Double flowers have purple corollas and cerise-red sepals. Best with some shelter in cold districts.
'**Eden Lady**' Half-hardy bedding fuchsia. Single flowers have pale violet-blue corollas veined with red and reddish-pink sepals. A good standard.
'**Estelle Marie**' Half-hardy bedding fuchsia. Single flowers have blue-violet corollas and white sepals. Holds its flowers erect.
'**Flying Cloud**' Half-hardy fuchsia suitable for a hanging basket. Double flowers have white corollas and sepals. A good double white cultivar.
'**Garden News**' Hardy fuchsia.

Fuchsias that have beautiful colored foliage, such as 'Autumnale,' are show-stoppers even before the flowers appear.

Semi-double flowers have magenta-red corollas and rose-pink sepals. A vigorous plant.

'Golden Dawn' Half-hardy bedding fuchsia. Single flowers have salmon-orange corollas and sepals. A good standard.

'Golden Marinka' Half-hardy fuchsia suitable for a hanging basket. Single flowers have red corollas and sepals. Golden leaves are veined with red.

'Golden Swingtime' Half-hardy fuchsia suitable for a hanging basket. Large double flowers have milk-white corollas and rich red sepals. Leaves are bright yellow-green.

'Harry Gray' Half-hardy fuchsia suitable for a hanging basket. Double flowers have white to pale pink corollas and white sepals tipped with green. Free-flowering.

'Heidi Ann' Half-hardy bedding fuchsia. Double flowers have bright lilac corollas and cerise-red sepals. A good standard.

'Hula Girl' Half-hardy fuchsia suitable for a hanging basket. Double flowers have white corollas and deep rose-pink sepals. Free-flowering.

'Jack Shahan' Half-hardy fuchsia suitable for a hanging basket. Large single flowers have pale to deep pink corollas and sepals. Free-flowering.

'Koralle' Frost tender triphylla-type bedding fuchsia. Flowers are rich orange. Makes an excellent specimen.

'La Campanella' Half-hardy fuchsia suitable for a hanging basket. Semi-double flowers have purple-blue corollas and white sepals. Free-flowering.

'Lady Thumb' Hardy fuchsia. Semi-double flowers have white corollas veined with pink and light red sepals. Good in a rock garden.

'Lena' Hardy fuchsia. Semi-double flowers have purple corollas and pale flesh-pink sepals. Free-flowering.

'Madame Cornelissen' Hardy fuchsia. Single flowers have white corollas veined with red and crimson sepals. Growth is upright.

magellanica Hardy species fuchsia. Single flowers have purple corollas and red sepals. Var. *molinae* has pale shell-pink flowers.

'Margaret' Hardy fuchsia. Double flowers have purple-violet corollas and crimson sepals. A good standard.

'Margaret Roe' Half-hardy

bedding fuchsia. Double flowers have pale violet-purple corollas and rose-red sepals. Flowers are held erect.

'Marin Glow' Half-hardy bedding fuchsia. Single flowers have purple-blue corollas and waxy white sepals. A good standard.

'Marinka' Half-hardy fuchsia suitable for a hanging basket. Single flowers have rich dark red corollas and slightly lighter red sepals. Leaves discolor in full sun.

'Mrs Popple' Hardy fuchsia. Single flowers have deep violet corollas and scarlet sepals. Suitable for a hedge.

'Mrs W Rundle' Half-hardy fuchsia suitable for a hanging basket. Large, long-tubed flowers have rich orange corollas and flesh-pink sepals. A good standard.

'Nellie Nuttall' Half-hardy bedding fuchsia. Single flowers have white corollas and red sepals. A good standard.

'Olive Smith' Half-hardy bedding fuchsia. Single flowers have rich crimson corollas and carmine-pink sepals. A good standard.

'Orange Drops' Half-hardy fuchsia suitable for a hanging basket. Single flowers have orange corollas and paler sepals. One of the best orange fuchsias.

'Pacquesa' Half-hardy bedding fuchsia. Single

■ BELOW
'Marinka' and 'Thalia' in a lead urn, the latter yet to flower but
distinguishable by its velvety leaves.

flowers have white corollas veined with red and deep red sepals. Free-flowering.

'**Peppermint Stick**' Half-hardy bedding fuchsia. Double flowers have rich purple corollas splashed with pink and carmine-red sepals. A good standard.

'**Phyllis**' Hardy fuchsia. Single flowers have crimson corollas and rose-red sepals. Suitable for a hedge.

'**Pink Galore**' Half-hardy fuchsia suitable for a hanging basket. Large double flowers have pale pink corollas and sepals. Flowers are borne terminally.

'**Pixie**' Hardy fuchsia. Single flowers have rose-mauve corollas veined with carmine-red and pale pink sepals. A vigorous, upright plant.

procumbens Half-hardy species fuchsia. Tiny flowers have yellow tubes and purple sepals. Grow in a rock garden or hanging basket.

'**Red Spider**' Half-hardy fuchsia suitable for a hanging basket. Single flowers have deep crimson corollas and paler sepals. A vigorous plant.

'**Riccartonii**' Hardy fuchsia. Small flowers have purple corollas and red petals. Suitable for a hedge.

'**Rose of Castile**' Hardy fuchsia. Small, single flowers have pink corollas flushed with purple and green-tipped

sepals. A good standard.

'**Rufus**' Half-hardy bedding fuchsia. Small, single flowers have red corollas and sepals. A good standard. Sometimes sold as 'Rufus the Red.'

'**Snowcap**' Half-hardy bedding fuchsia. Single flowers have white corollas and bright red sepals. Free-flowering.

'**Strawberry Delight**' Half-hardy fuchsia suitable for a hanging basket. Double flowers have white corollas veined pink and crimson sepals. Leaves are yellowish-green overlaid with bronze.

'**Susan Travis**' Hardy fuchsia. Single flowers are rose-pink, the sepals tipped with green. Makes a rounded bush.

'**Swingtime**' Half-hardy fuchsia suitable for a hanging basket. Large, double flowers have milk-white corollas and rich red sepals. A good standard.

'**Temple Bells**' Hardy fuchsia. Single flowers have mauve corollas and red sepals. An upright plant.

'**Tennessee Waltz**' Hardy fuchsia. Semi-double flowers have soft lilac corollas and

rose-pink sepals. A good standard.

'**Texas Longhorn**' Half-hardy fuchsia suitable for a hanging basket. Very large, double flowers have white corollas veined red and wide-spreading red sepals. A good standard.

'**Thalia**' Frost tender triphylla-type bedding fuchsia. Flowers are rich orange-red. Grow in full sun.

'**Trase**' Hardy fuchsia. Semi-double or double flowers have white corollas flushed deep pink and cerise-red sepals. Upright habit.

'**Tristesse**' Half-hardy bedding fuchsia. Double flowers have pale mauve corollas and pink sepals tipped with green. A good standard.

'**Westminster Chimes**' Half-hardy fuchsia suitable for a hanging basket. Semi-double flowers have bluish-violet corollas and rose-pink sepals. Free-flowering.

'**White Ann**' Half-hardy bedding fuchsia. Double flowers have white corollas veined with red and red sepals. Makes a good standard.

'**White Spider**' Half-hardy fuchsia suitable for a hanging basket. Single flowers have white corollas veined with pink and pale pink sepals tipped with green. A good standard.

Index

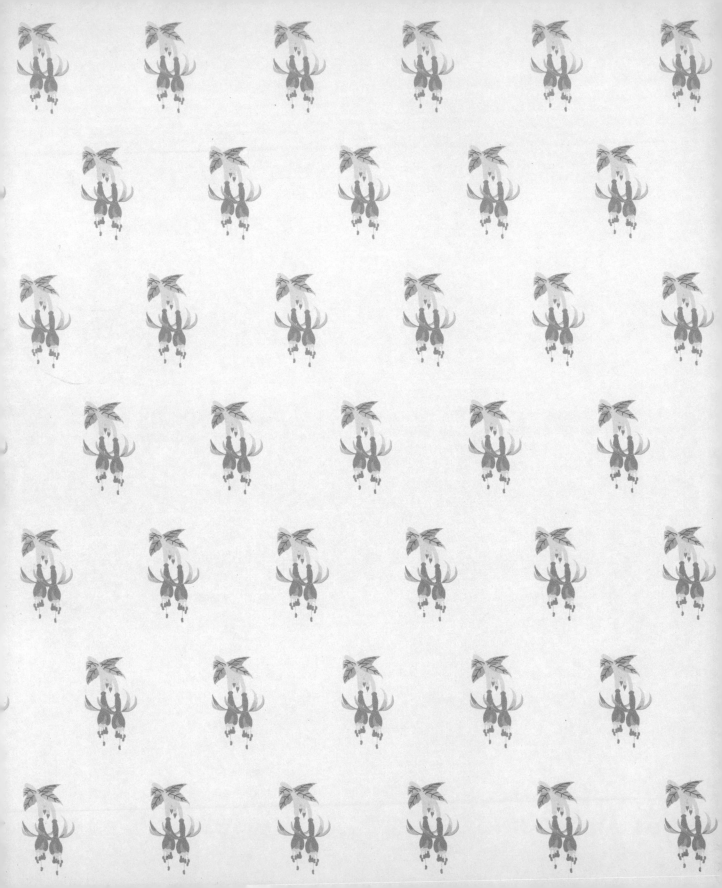